THAT'S STRANGE!

SECRETS OF THE SPHINX

Tim Cooke

Lerner Publications ◆ Minneapolis

Copyright © 2025 by Lerner Publishing Group, Inc.

All rights reserved. International copyright secured. No part of this book may be reproduced, stored in a retrieval system, or transmitted in any form or by any means—electronic, mechanical, photocopying, recording, or otherwise—without the prior written permission of Lerner Publishing Group, Inc., except for the inclusion of brief quotations in an acknowledged review.

Lerner Publications Company
An imprint of Lerner Publishing Group, Inc.
241 First Avenue North
Minneapolis, MN 55401 USA

For reading levels and more information, look up this title at www.lernerbooks.com.

Main body text set in ITC Franklin Gothic.
Typeface provided by International Typeface Corporation.

Library of Congress Cataloging-in-Publication Data

Names: Cooke, Tim, 1961- author.
Title: Secrets of the Sphinx / Tim Cooke.
Description: Minneapolis : Lerner Publications, [2025] | Series: That's strange! : Updog books |Includes bibliographical references and index. | Audience: Ages 8–11 | Audience: Grades 4–6 |
Summary: "A giant statue of a lion with a human head sits in the Egyptian desert. Who built the Sphinx? Does it have the face of a king? Readers will learn about the Sphinx"— Provided by publisher.
Identifiers: LCCN 2024015159 (print) | LCCN 2024015160 (ebook) | ISBN 9798765648209 (library binding) | ISBN 9798765662540 (paperback) | ISBN 9798765658918 (epub)
Subjects: LCSH: Great Sphinx (Egypt)—Juvenile literature. | Egypt—Antiquities—Juvenile literature.
Classification: LCC DT62.S7 C66 2025 (print) | LCC DT62.S7 (ebook) | DDC 932/.2—dc23/eng/20240405

LC record available at https://lccn.loc.gov/2024015159
LC ebook record available at https://lccn.loc.gov/2024015160

Manufactured in the United States of America

1 – CG – 12/15/24

Table of Contents

Buried!   4

Who Built the Sphinx?   8

Lost in the Sand   18

Questions   24

Glossary   30

Check It Out!   31

Index   32

Buried!

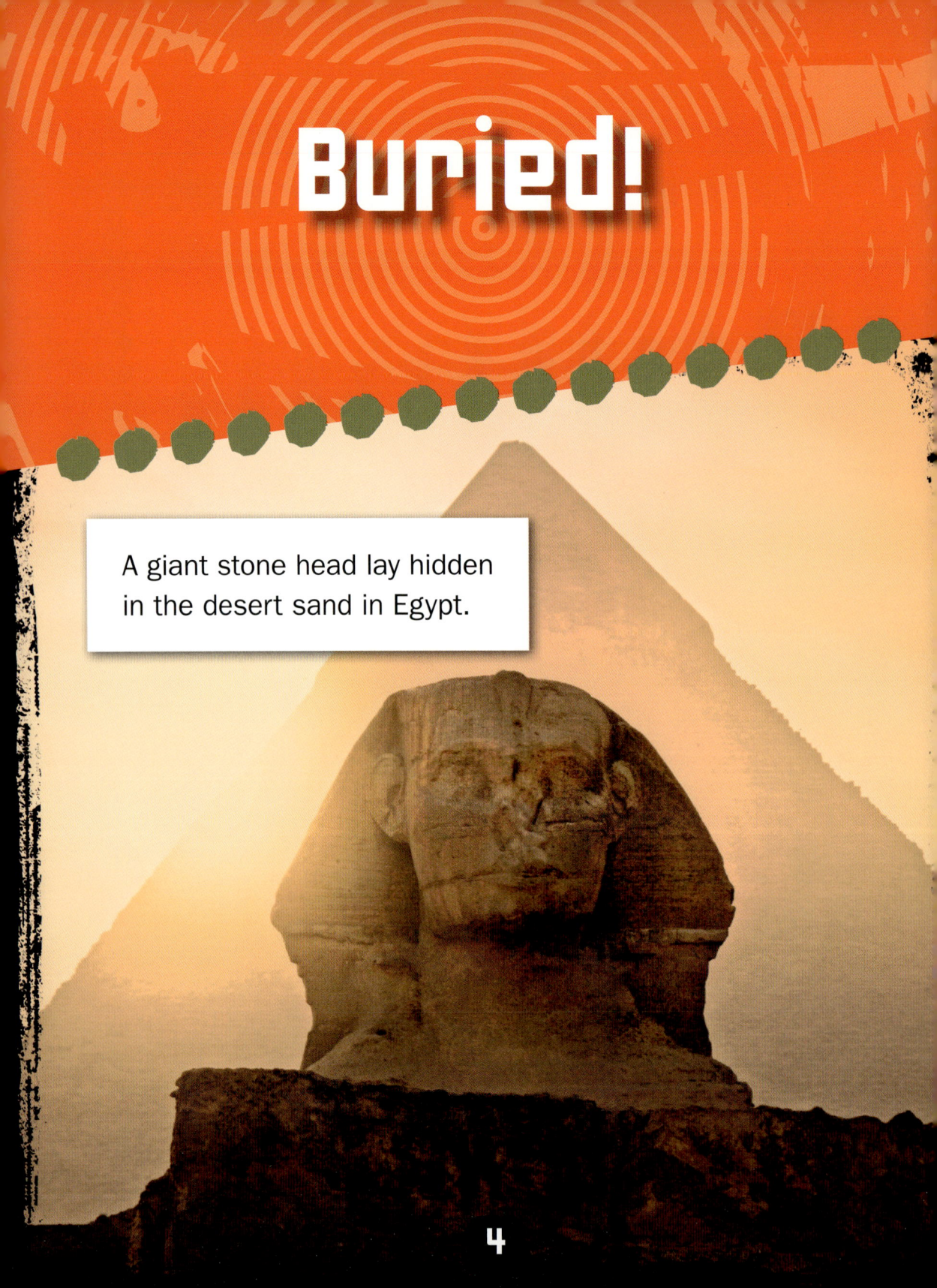

A giant stone head lay hidden in the desert sand in Egypt.

It was near three tall pyramids.

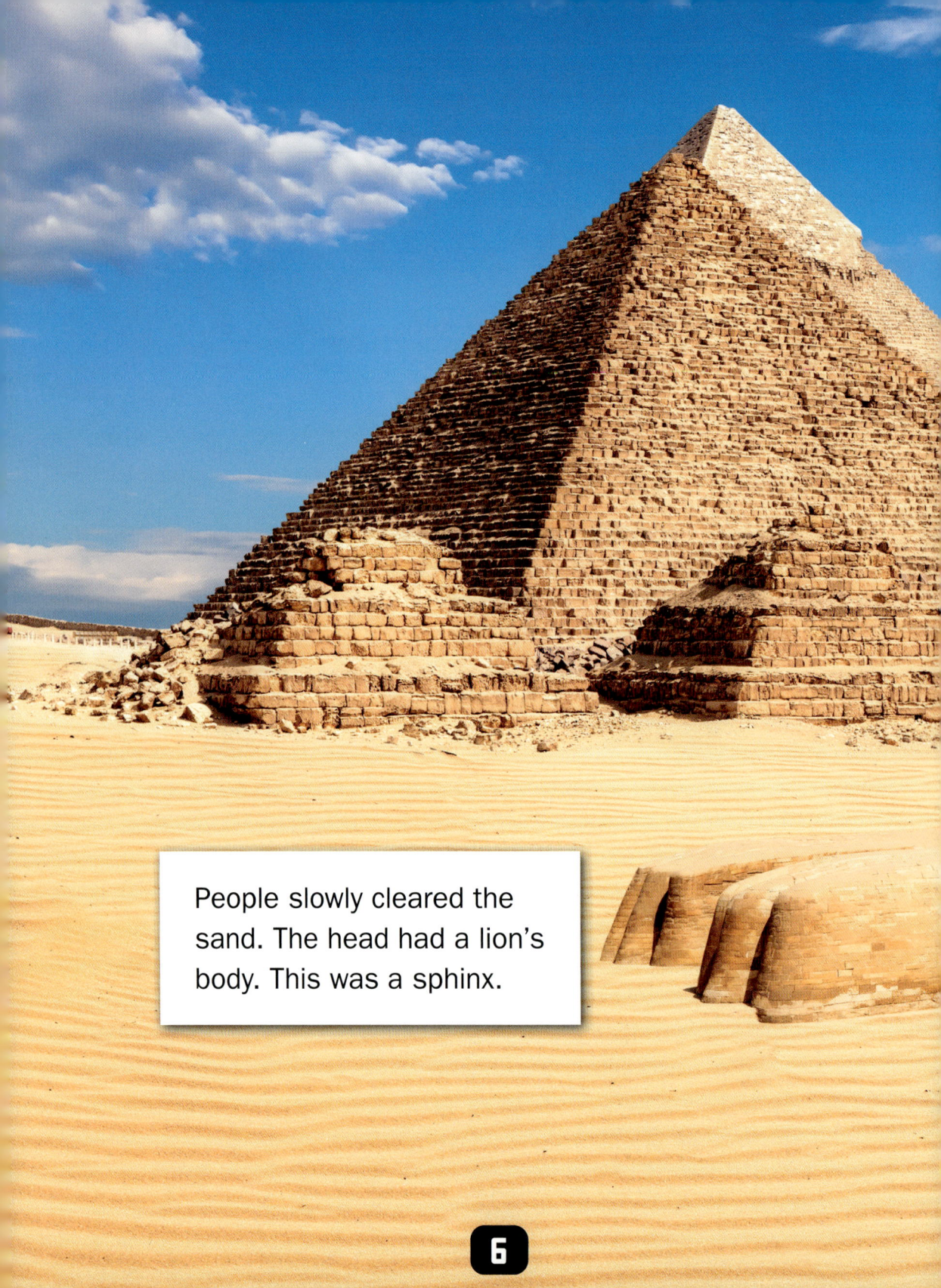

People slowly cleared the sand. The head had a lion's body. This was a sphinx.

UP NEXT!

MYSTERY BUILDERS.

Who Built the Sphinx?

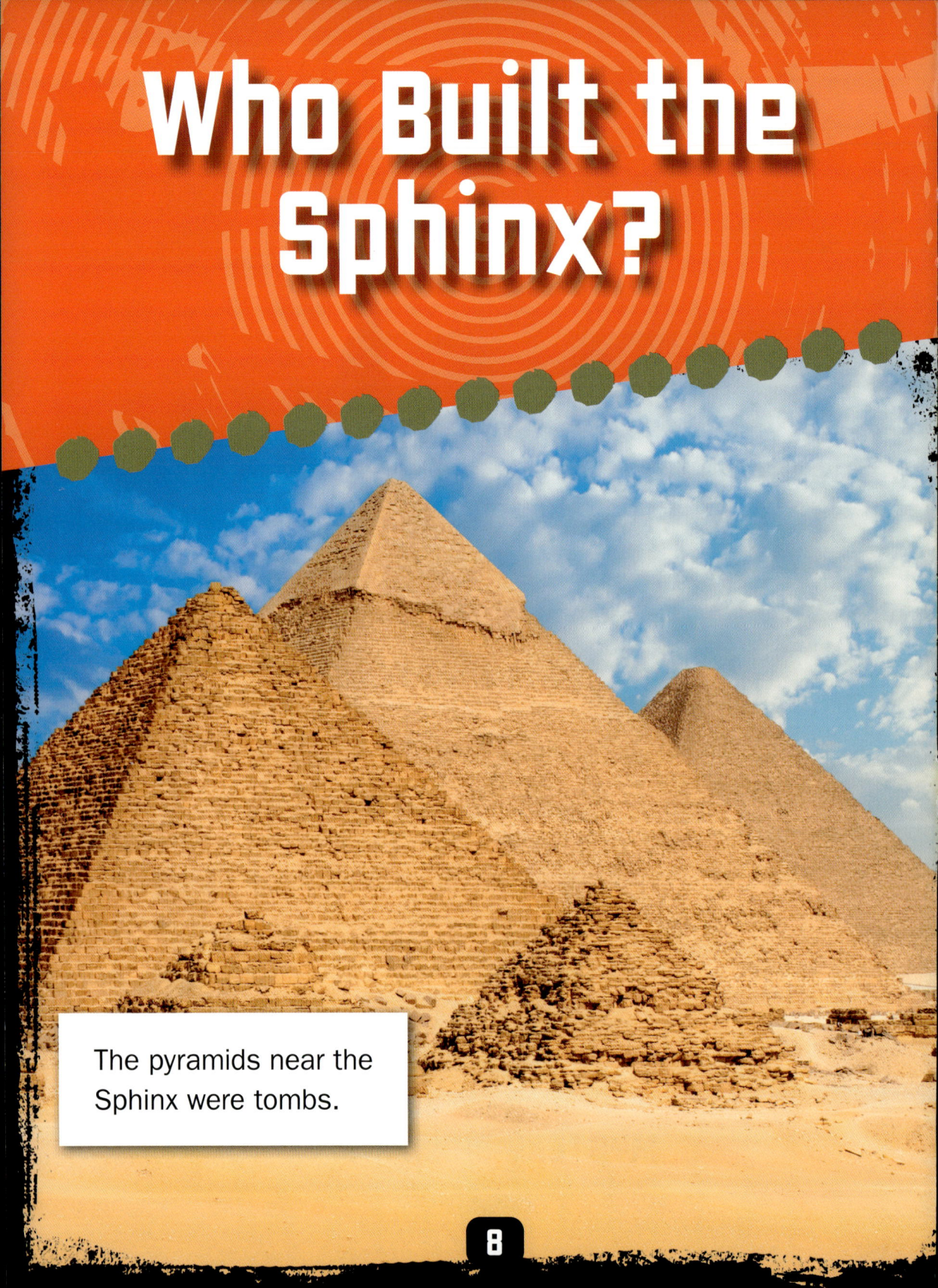

The pyramids near the Sphinx were tombs.

They were built by the kings of ancient Egypt.

The Great Pyramid was built by Pharaoh Khufu.

It is more than 4,000 years old.

Inside the Great Pyramid

It took 20 years to build the Great Pyramid.

The workers lived in a city nearby. They worked night and day.

The workers' city

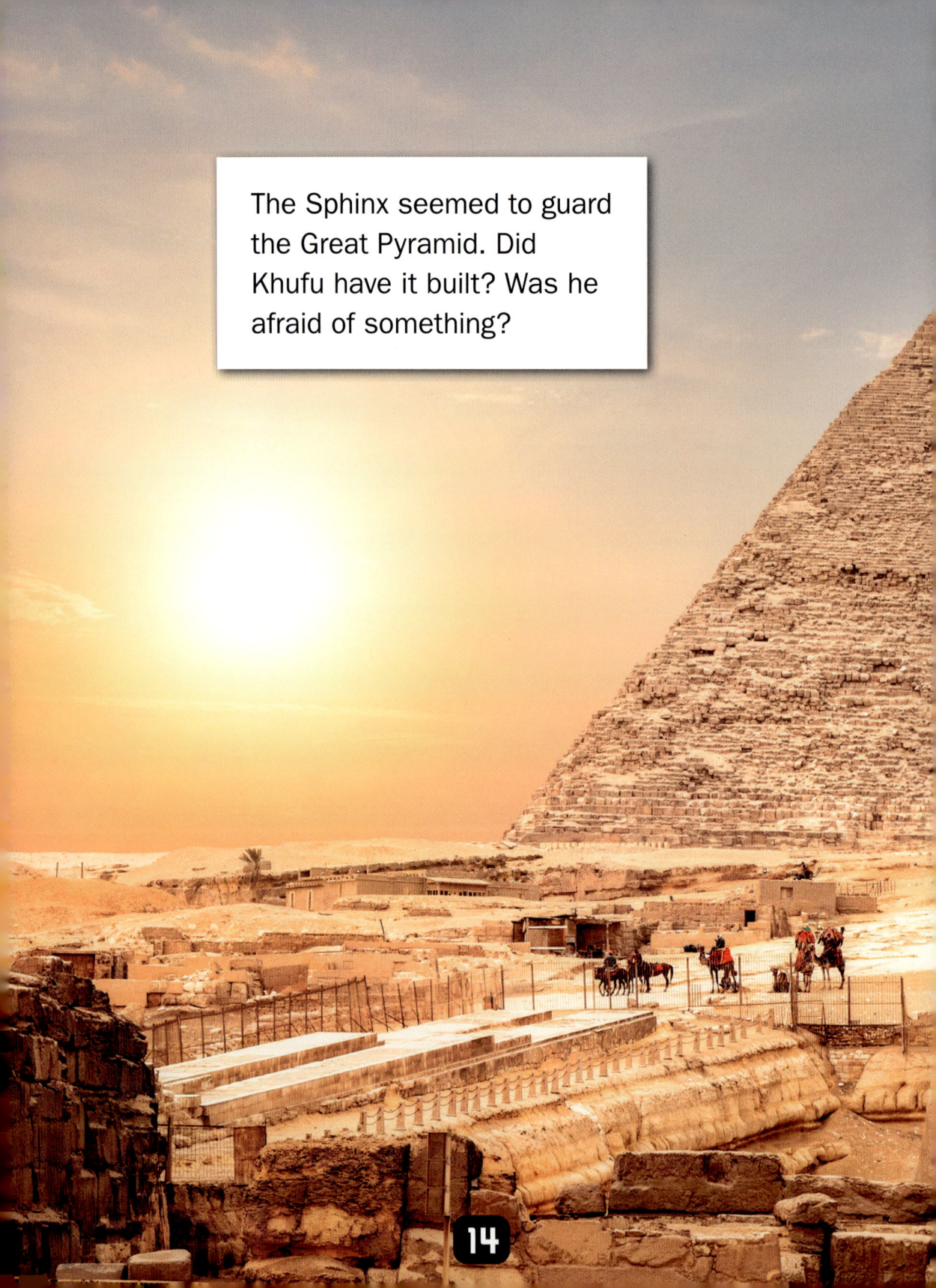

The Sphinx seemed to guard the Great Pyramid. Did Khufu have it built? Was he afraid of something?

List Break!

Monuments near the Sphinx:

The Pyramid of Khufu, or the Great Pyramid

The Pyramid of Khafre

The Pyramid of Menkaure and the Queens' Pyramids

The Temple of Rameses

Temples

Lost in the Sand

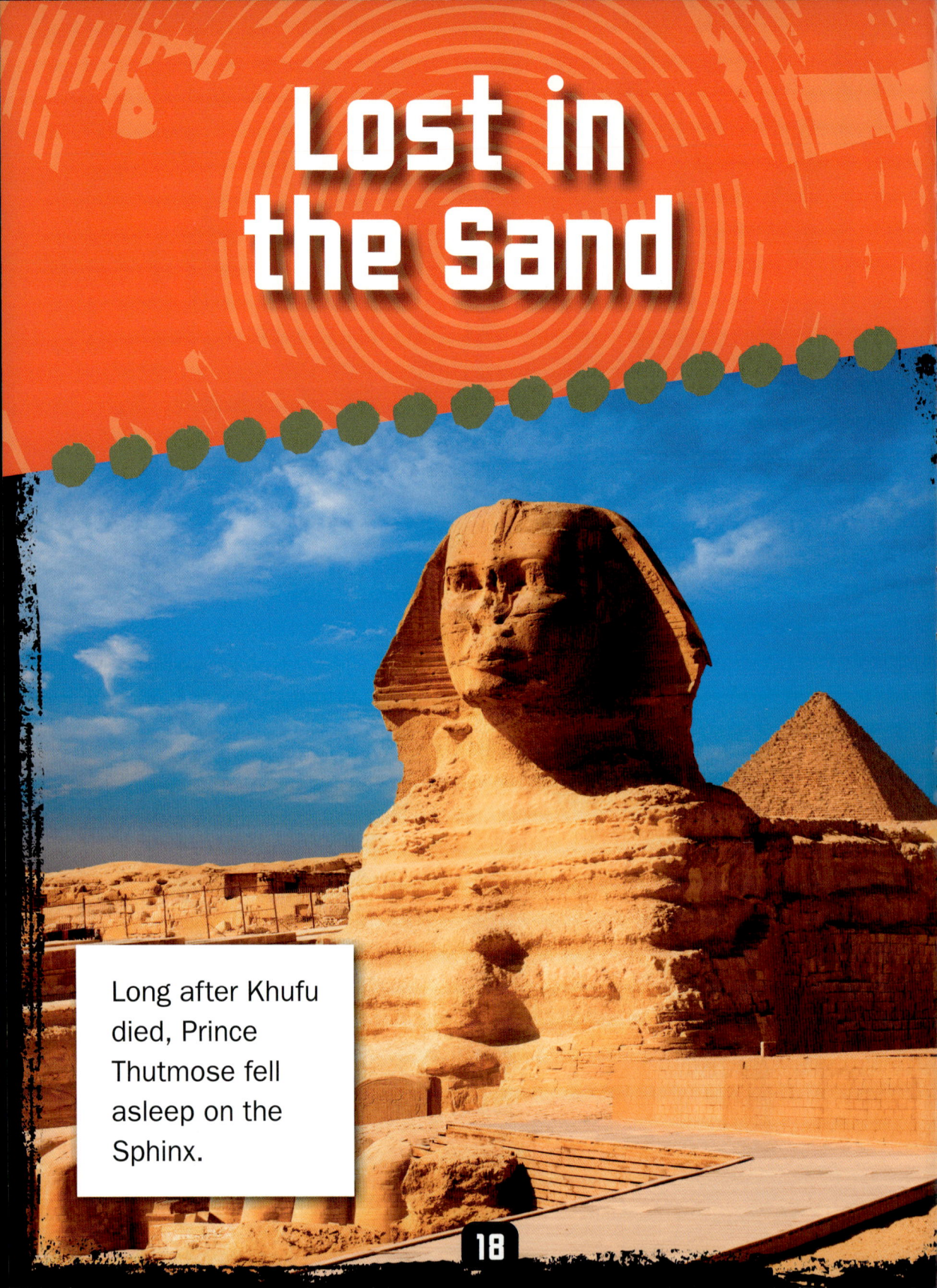

Long after Khufu died, Prince Thutmose fell asleep on the Sphinx.

In a dream, the Sphinx told Thutmose he would become pharaoh.

Story of Thutmose's dream

Thutmose became pharaoh.

He made the Egyptians worship the Sphinx.

After Thutmose died, the Sphinx was forgotten. It was covered by sand.

All that could be seen was its head.

UP NEXT!

WHAT DO WE KNOW?

Questions

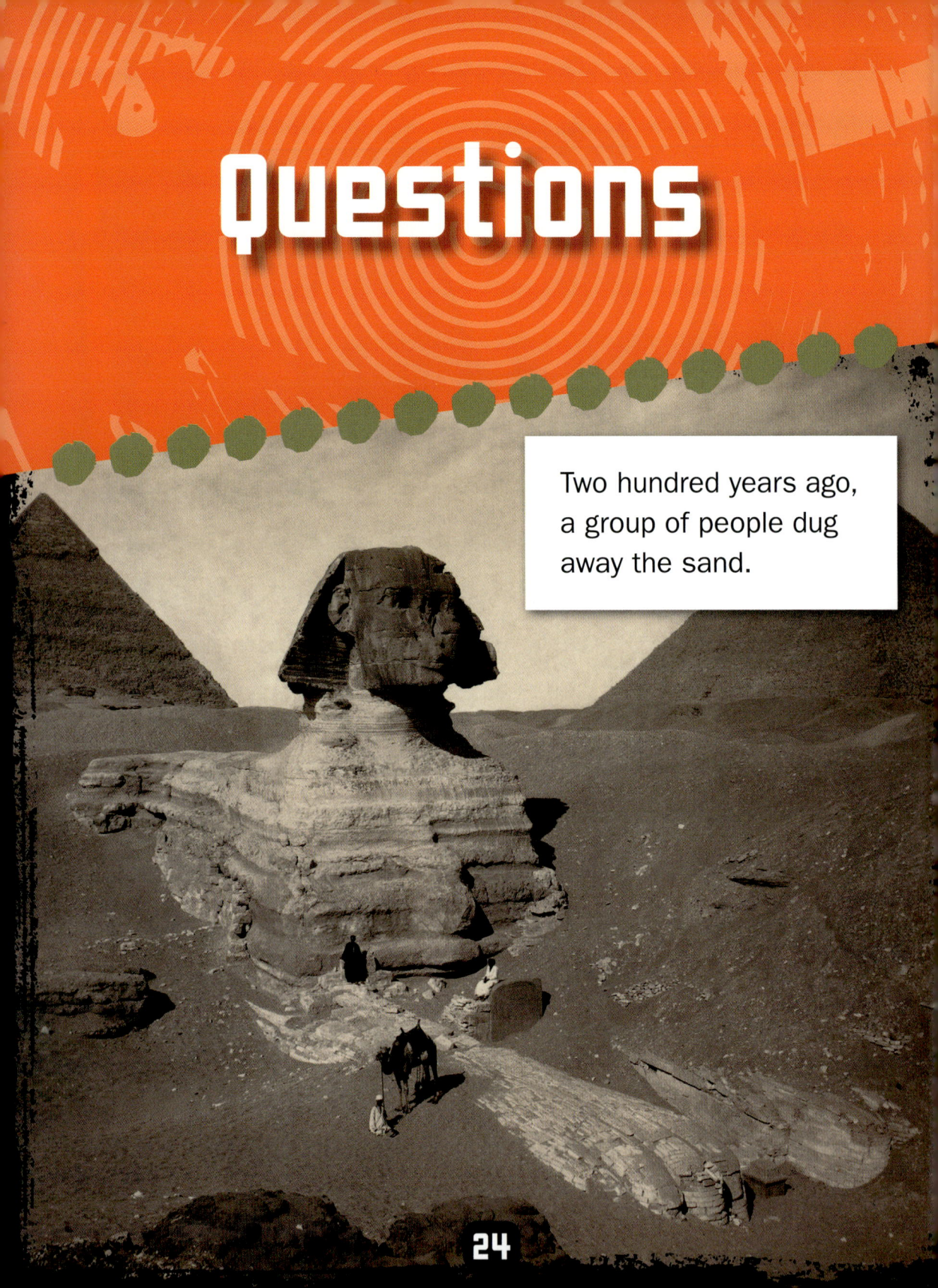

Two hundred years ago, a group of people dug away the sand.

They revealed the Sphinx.

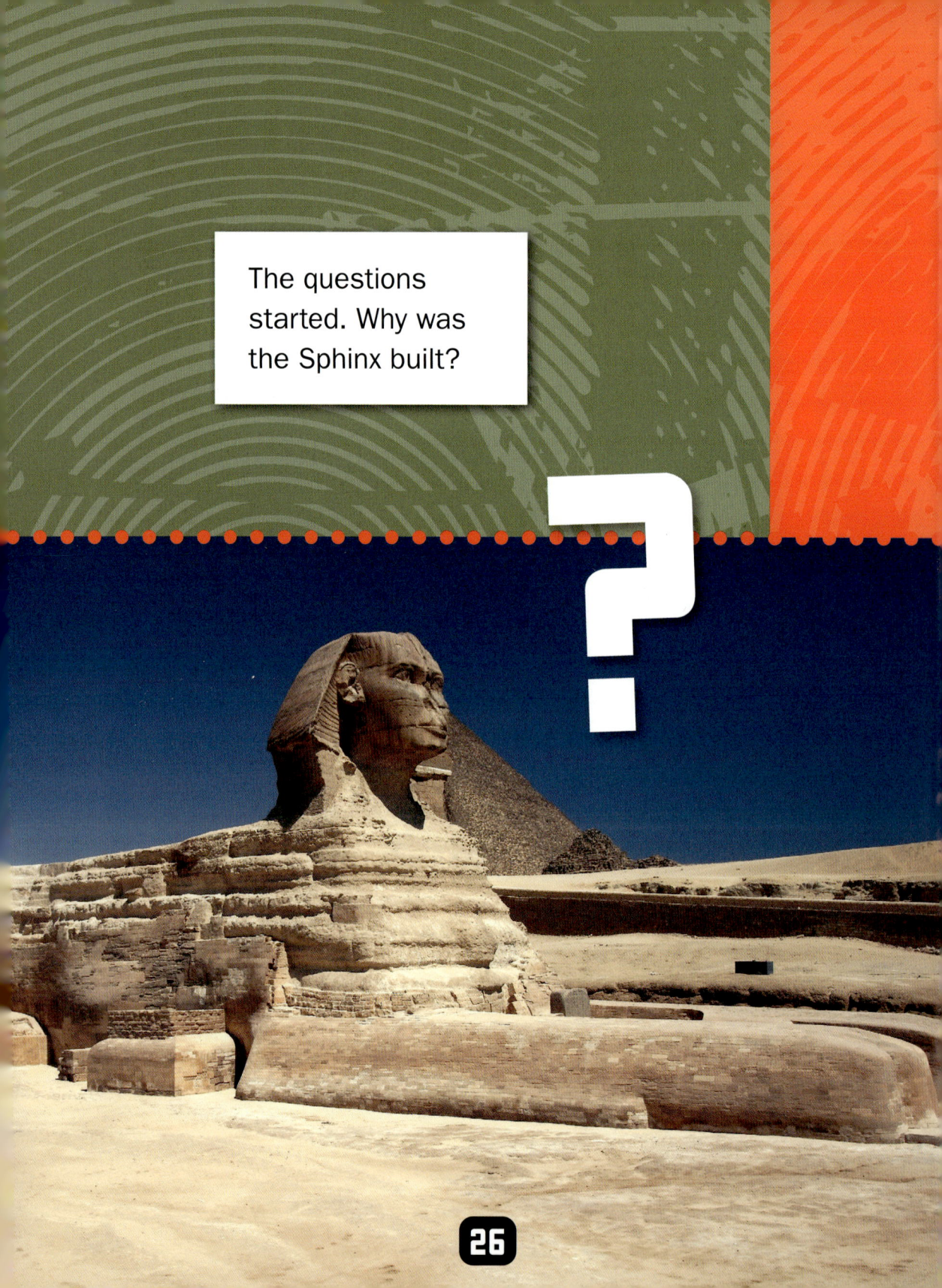

The questions started. Why was the Sphinx built?

Did Khufu build it?

Is the Sphinx's face a picture of Khufu? What was the Sphinx really for?

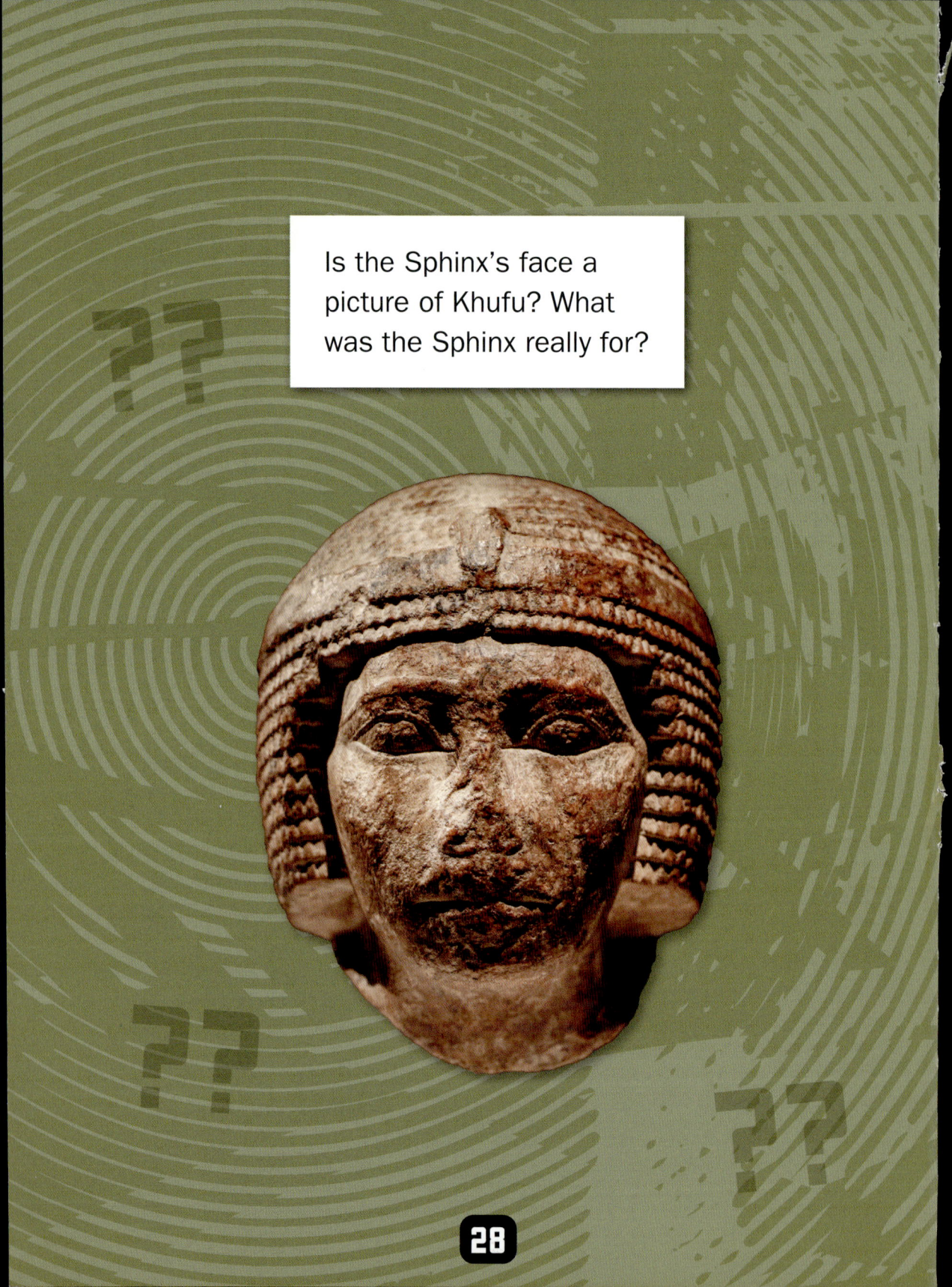

Nobody knows for sure.

Glossary

ancient: very old

desert: a dry area that gets very little rain

pharaoh: a king of ancient Egypt

pyramid: a building with a square base and triangular sides that meet in a point at the top

tombs: places to keep dead bodies

worship: to show love for a god or goddess

Check It Out!

Academic Kids: Sphinx
https://academickids.com/encyclopedia/index.php/Sphinx

Ha, Christine. *Sphinx*. Mendota Heights, MN: Apex, 2022.

Kiddle: Great Sphinx Facts for Kids
https://kids.kiddle.co/The_Great_Sphinx

Oachs, Emily Rose. *Ancient Egypt*. Minneapolis: Bellwether Media, 2020.

O'Neill, Sean. *50 Things You Didn't Know About Ancient Egypt*. South Egremont, MA: Red Chair Press, 2020.

Social Studies for Kids: Giza: Site of the Sphinx and the Pyramids
https://socialstudiesforkids.com/articles/worldhistory/giza.htm

Index

Egypt, 4, 9

Great Pyramid, 10–11, 12, 14, 16

Khufu, 10, 14, 16, 18, 27, 28

lion, 6

pyramid, 5, 8, 10–11, 12, 14, 16

Thutmose, 18–19, 20, 22

Photo Acknowledgments

Image credits: Pius Lee/Dreamstime.com, pp. 3, 18; R raymoonds/Shutterstock, p. 4; Sergii Kolesnyk/Dreamstime.com, p. 5; AlexAnton/Shutterstock, pp. 6–7, 14–15; Daily Travel Photos/Shutterstock, p. 8; Jaroslav Moravcik/Shutterstock, p. 9; Mikhail Nekrasov /dreamstime.com, p. 10; WitthayaP/Shutterstock, p. 11; Everett Collection/Shutterstock, p. 12; Delpixel/Shutterstock, p. 13; ImAAm/Shutterstock, p. 16 (top); Romantiche/Dreamstime.com, p. 16(bottom); Anton Ibanov/Shutterstock, p. 17 (top); Quintanilla/Shutterstock, p. 17 (bottom); Petr Bonner/Shutterstock, p. 19; Markh/English Wikipedia Project, p. 20; Gift of Egypt Exploration Fund, 1907/Metropolitan Museum of Art, p. 21; Nicram Sabod/Shutterstock p. 22; Baloncici/Shutterstock, p. 23; Library of Congress, p. 24; Metropolitan Museum of Art/Wikimedia Commons, p. 25; GFDL/Wikimedia Commons, p. 26; Claudio Caridi/Shutterstock, p. 27; Archaioptix/Wikipedia, p. 28; Aarstudio/dreamstime.com, p. 29: Design elements: sokolovski/Shutterstock, pp. 1–32.

Cover: sokolovski/Shutterstock; Pius Lee/Dreamstime.com; Olaf Tausch/Wikimedia Commons.